Ambushed by Grief

A survival guide for the early shock of bereavement

By

Eloise Cowherd, M. Div.
And
Toni Griffith, LCSW

Open Door
Publications

ISBN: 978-0-9838750-9-3

Published by
Open Door Publications
27 Carla Way
Lawrenceville, NJ 08648
www.OpenDoorPublications.com

Cover and Interior Design by
Michelle Helfrich
MH Design Company, LLC
Cherry Hill, NJ

CONTENTS:
FRAGMENTS, FINDINGS,
INSIGHTS & MEANDERINGS

There is little discernible order to the contents of this guide any more than there is an orderly progression to your life when you have been ambushed by grief. But here, for your convenience, are listed in the order of their appearance, the assorted fragments, findings, insights and meanderings in this book.

THE ASSORTMENT

Dedicated to

ELLIE'S LIST

My Mother

My Father

My Grandparents

My Sister Lori

My Brother-in-Law Frank

My Nephew Kent

My Nephew Bart

My Great Nephew Kyle

Many Aunts, Uncles,

Cousins,

Congregants…

TONI'S LIST

John Michael Pitale
for 26 years of proofreading,
love and support

Mom and Dad

Griff and Alicia

Grandparents

The many Aunts
and Uncles

Patricia

Bernice and Robert

The AIDS Family…

…Friends and Associates,
and the sea of faces,
the chorus of voices,
known now only in
fond memory and
gentle gratitude,
because they have taught us that…

> ## "…suddenly with no warning you are ambushed by grief."
>
> *To Bless the Space between Us, A Book of Blessings,*
> by John O'Donahue, Doubleday, New York. 2008

Dear Reader,

We are sorry for your loss.

We know that's easy to say. And it doesn't begin to touch the ache that you feel, but we truly are sorry and we would like to help.

Sadly, there are no words that can take away your pain. Please know that we understand that. We know that the two things you desperately want are:

> **Most important:**
>> **to have your loved one back**
>
> **Or at least:**
>> **to have the hurt stop**

These are the very things that no one can give you.

Your loss has set you on a strange and

painful journey into the unexpected reality

of bereavement.

The private world of grief has a different orbit of

time . . .

...before death

...after death

Holidays are not welcome. Sunshine isn't cheerful. Things disappear and you don't know where they went. (Why are the keys in the refrigerator?)

We offer this little book with the hope that it will help and be a support for you. Please use this book as a guide in any way you choose.

There are pages you may want to keep and pages you will throw away.

Some pages are for you to write, draw or doodle on…if you feel like doing it. There are also some fill-in-the-blanks pages. And some pages just for you to read and think about,

…and maybe even argue with.

It's okay to skip around, and also read

the last page first if you want.

You're in control here

and we honor your spirit.

With our best wishes,

Ellie
&
Toni

Ellie and Toni

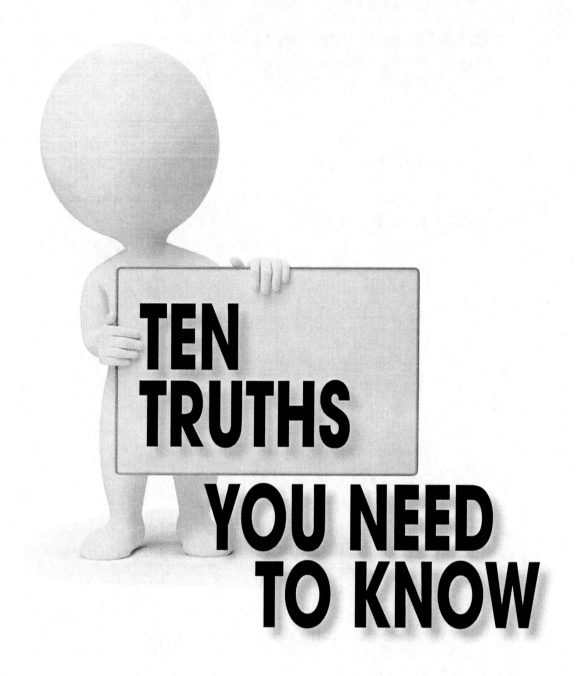

10

Alcohol and drugs
are no substitute for
chocolate and hugs.

9

No one can make
the pain end before
it's time. Grief has
its own agenda.

8

You can't live in the past.
Time only moves forward.
Eventually you have to go to the
bathroom. And at some point,
you have to eat and sleep.

7

You will find out who understands
and who doesn't (yet).

6

You are not going crazy. It's normal to hear him, see her, and sense their presence.

5

Making lists doesn't help if you lose the lists.

4

You have an indestructible core
and an unquenchable flame, but you
don't know who you are right now.

3

You may think you have lost your faith, but your faith has not let go of you.

2

You will never forget.

1

You will survive.

Belonging —
A Lament

You belong to me.

You belong to us.

We belong to each other.

You can't have left us.

You belong here.

It feels so strange, unreal.

I can't believe this

You can't not be here.

This is where you belong.

I never realized we were so connected.

The circle is broken.

There is an empty space now.

Somebody cut my heart out.

What are we going to do now?

You belonged to us.

We've been robbed.

NOBODY GRIEVES THE SAME WAY

Are you in deep anguish?
– **that's normal**.

Are you not so much feeling grieved, but that you would like to punch a hole in someone or something? – **that's normal too**.

Are you only experiencing a mild sense of disorientation? – **that's normal too**.

Are you feeling like there's a lead weight on your heart? – **that's normal too**.

Are you experiencing only occasional moments of sadness? – **that's normal too**.

Are you like a yo-yo – up and down with all or some of those experiences?

– **that's normal too**.

Normal doesn't mean it doesn't hurt

Normal doesn't mean you wouldn't benefit from some help or support

Normal just means…this is the way it goes.

What else is normal?

Well, maybe you have trouble sleeping.

Maybe you're not eating well – or too well.

Are you numb? Does your body hurt?

Are you hyper?

Are you out of steam?

Normal.

Are you caught between how you think you should grieve and doing it your way?

Is it hard to focus?

Is there sometimes a lot of turmoil inside you?

Are you daydreaming more than usual?

Are you often irritated with everyone and everything?

Do you wish people could just understand what you're going through?

Normal.

Do you want to pull the covers over your head and not get up in the morning?

Or are you keeping really busy?

Normal.

Well, there. You get the idea.

A wide range of emotions, experiences, reactions…all a part of grieving.

So don't be surprised by what ambushes you.

Take a look at Grief Zingo on the next page. See how much of it relates to you today.

GRIEFZINGO

INSTRUCTIONS: Cross off any box that applies to you. You get ZINGO when you have crossed off five boxes, across, up and down, or diagonally. If you get ZINGO, you need chocolate, or a hug.

	G	R	I	E	F
Z	I couldn't sleep last night	I couldn't find my keys	Everybody irritates me today	I missed a meal – I didn't feel like eating	I keep wondering why
I	I feel like there's a lead weight on my heart	I am so angry at God	I'm amazed at how kind people are	I can't seem to get organized	I actually laughed at something today
N	I'm trying to be strong for my family	I'm dreading the next big holiday	I cried today	I couldn't find my keys again	I don't feel like socializing
G	I keep wondering, what if	I didn't feel like getting up and dressed today	I'm getting tired of all these casseroles	I wish people wouldn't try to cheer me up	I can't seem to focus on anything
O	Someone was very helpful to me/us today	I wish this pain would stop	I can't seem to get interested in anything	I'm not sure what I believe in anymore	I cried again today

13 MYTHS
about GRIEF

MYTH: 1
You'll get over it in no time at all
*** not necessarily so ***

MYTH: 2
Time heals all wounds
*** maybe not all of them ***

MYTH: 3
Keeping busy is important
*** doing nothing is okay ***

MYTH: 4
Crying is a sign of weakness
*** No way. It's one of your strengths ***

MYTH: 5
You should leave all that baggage behind you
*** not necessarily so ***

MYTH: 6
God needed another angel in heaven
*** Nope. God doesn't work that way. ***

MYTH: 7
It's best to put away the pictures
*** Leave them out.
Treasure your memories. ***

MYTH: 8

You should stop talking about your loved one – it only makes it worse

*** No. It helps. ***

MYTH: 9

The first month is the hardest

*** Not necessarily. Every step along the way has its challenges ***

MYTH: 10

Things will be back to normal soon

*** Forward to a different normal, when the time is right. ***

MYTH: 11

Grief always brings families together and heals old wounds

** *Only in the movies and very fortunate families* **

MYTH: 12

A good stiff drink will help

** *Probably not.* **

MYTH: 13

Pills too

** *The pain will still be there.* **

I HAVE TO TELL THEM
ABOUT YOU

I find myself talking about you all the time.
I have to make people understand
how wonderful you were – how you were loved.

It's like a sacred urgency.
Maybe I can keep you alive if everyone knows.
Maybe I can keep your spirit alive in anyone who
will listen.

I can't bring you back.
But I can tell the world who you were.
You mattered. You matter now.

I tell the world the best of you.
I want the world to know what it has lost.

I never want to forget what I have lost.
Who I have lost.

I will keep telling them about you.

What I Miss Right Now

I miss hearing

I miss seeing

I miss tasting

I miss smelling

I miss touching

I want people to remember _____

_____

I will never forget _____

_____

_____

If only I could talk to you one more time, I would
say_____

_____

_____

I would tell you I'm sorry for_____

_____

_____

I would say I forgive you for _____

_____

_____

_____

I miss you. I miss you. I miss you so.
Thank you for being in my life!

I NEED TO SAY IT AGAIN AND AGAIN!

Thank you for being in my life!

People are sharing wonderful memories of you.

Let me share some of mine with you.

You always _____

_____

_____

I remember when you _____

_____

_____

I was grateful _____

_____

_____

I remember the day _____

_____

_____

You taught me _____

_____

We laughed about _____

_____

_____

There were some rough times_____

_____

We survived _____

_____

_____

My happiest memory is _____

_____

_____

_____

I cherish _____

_____

Thank you for being in my life!

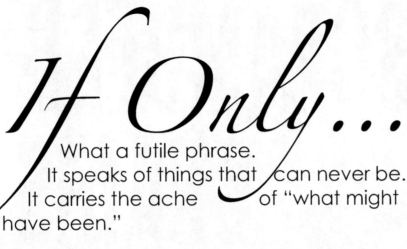

If Only...

What a futile phrase.
It speaks of things that can never be.
It carries the ache of "what might have been."

Never again will you light up the room with
    your welcoming smile.
Never again will your gifts dazzle us.
Now the world will never see what you might
    have become.
Your gifts have been buried with you.
But they still live on in my memories of you.
If only they could breathe again.

If only we could hear you play the piano once again.
If only the sound of your voice could be heard again.
If only you could make us laugh again.
If only we could savor your presence once more.
If only we could cheer your successes yet again.
If only we could revel in the miracle that was you.

If only . . .

From "Maud Muller" by John Greenleaf Whittier (1807-1892)
    For of all sad words of tongue or pen,

The saddest are these: "It might have been!"

SCRAMBLED BRAINS

I feel like I'm going crazy...

because I can't

remember anything...

because I want people to come and visit,
but I want them to leave me alone...

because I lost the check book and I keep
forgetting to look for it...

because I can't recognize my
signature on the checks anyway...

because I can't stand to be alone,
but I don't want to leave the house...

because sunshine and the sound of laughter make me sad...

because sunshine and the sound of laughter
make me mad as hell...

because I just can't focus...

because I just put the milk in the cupboard
and the keys in the refrigerator...

SCRAMBLED BRAINS

because I'm just not me...

and I don't know who I am...

Did you find yourself in those lines?

This is the way

your brain works

(or doesn't) in grief.

It really is very normal.

But it doesn't feel

normal, or even sane.

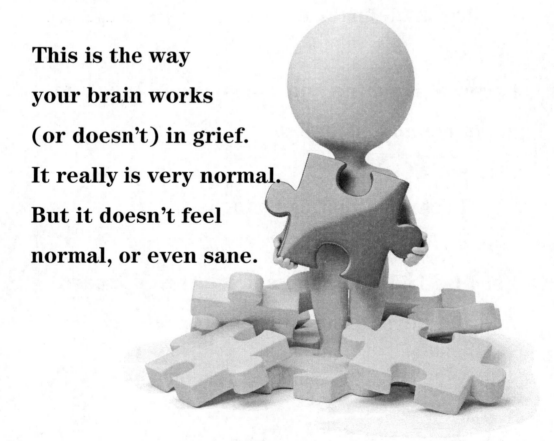

Scrambled brains have great difficulty with decisions. It might seem like the wisest thing in the world to do but later you discover it wasn't.

What to keep and what to get rid of...

When to enter a new relationship...with whom?

Keep or sell the house?

Buy a new car?

Throw away his/her collections?

Trash all the pictures?
...Display all the pictures?

SCRAMBLED BRAINS

Get out of bed today?

...Get out of bed AND
get dressed today?

......Get out of bed
AND get dressed
AND go outside today?

Buy all new
furniture?

Mow the yard?

Eat...Or not?

Move?

Move in with the kids?

Pay bills, or taxes?

Shop like mad...
Return everything?

Get high, get drunk, get stoned?

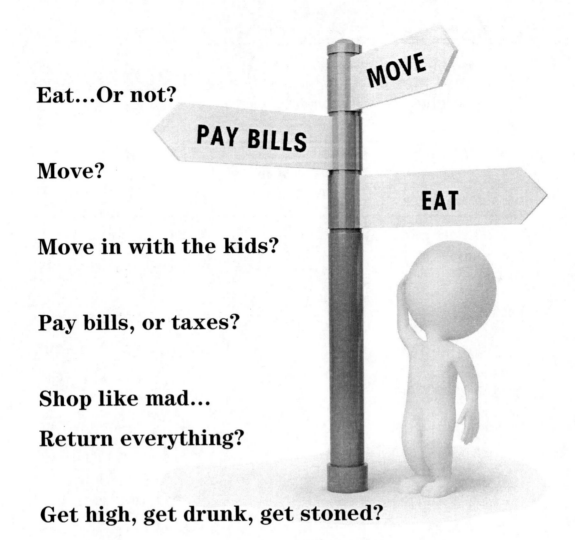

Scrambled brains have a lot of internal and external clutter

Clutter, clutter, *everywhere!*

Well of course there is. Our outside world often matches our inside world.

EXTERNAL Is this what it's like?	Can you connect the clutter with the cause(s)?	**INTERNAL** Because
Papers and magazines everywhere		I just can't focus
		My mind jumps from one thing to another
Piles of junk mail		I couldn't care less
Laundry piling up		I don't have any energy
Stuff everywhere		I wouldn't have to do all this if you were here.
Unpaid bills		Every time I start to do things, I start to cry
Trash is piling up		I just can't seem to make even small decisions
The dishes aren't done		I just sit and stare
Spider webs		It's not important anymore because you're not here
What can you add to this list?		What can you add to this list?
_____		_____
_____		_____
_____		_____

The
Guilt
of Paralysis

I know I should get up and do something.

I should exercise. I should eat something.

My shoes don't match.

I might go to the store if I ever find
the car keys. But not today.

There are calls I should make.
Notes I should write. Emails I
should answer. Stuff I should do.

I'm just paralyzed. What's wrong
with me? This isn't like me. I'm afraid
I'll never get back to normal.

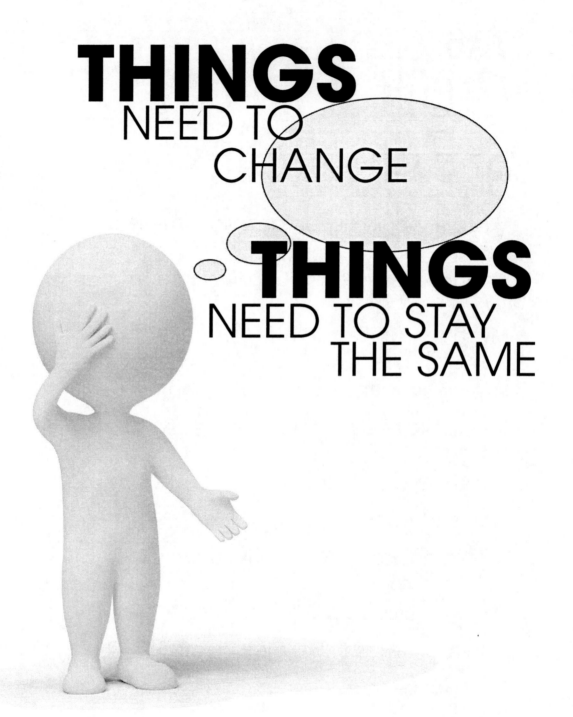

This space, this place I call
home has so much of
all of us in every
corner.
 I see you,
but you are
only there
in the things
that are still
there...

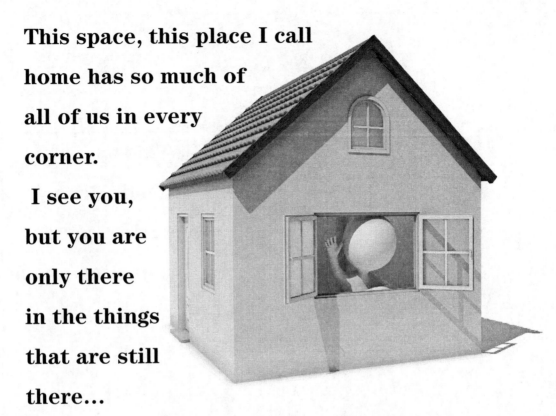

Do those things have to stay
forever in the same spot...Some of
them make me cry, make me
remember and I want to put them
away, give them away, take them
away. Some of them I want to hold
and care for always.

This space needs decorating, needs painting, needs rearranging, needs updating... Dare I move things, change things, put things in that only I like and want to live with???

Should I get the
fence fixed?

I think an alarm system
might be wise.

Who do I call about
putting in railings
on the steps?

Would I like
to redo
the living
room with
blue and
crème?

Your WOUNDED Spirit

"Some days it just CRUSHES ME."

"O Lord, why didn't I get a miracle?

We prayed so hard."

We DIDN'T DESERVE THIS.

"What soul? I don't think I have a soul anymore."

"DAMN GOD! I know it's taboo

to say that, but that's how I feel!"

"It's like someone just reached in and CUT A

BIG CHUNK OUT OF MY INSIDES."

"EVERYBODY IS TRYING TO TELL ME 'WHY' and 'he's in a better place' and a lot of other nonsense I don't believe."

"WHY DIDN'T MY PRAYERS WORK?"

"GOD, HELP ME! I don't think I can get through this without you."

"I don't give a damn if God needed another angel in heaven. I WANT HER HERE. Right here. With me."

"If only I had believed more, PRAYED MORE."

"GOD IS NOT MY FRIEND
and I'm not speaking to him."

"THERE IS NO GOD
There are no answers."

"I always believed that if we

live well and honor God…

WE WILL BE PROTECTED . . . "

I DON'T GO TO
CHURCH/TEMPLE
ANY MORE.

Weren't we good enough for
GOD TO HEAR US?

"I know GOD IS WITH ME. I couldn't
get through this without MY FAITH."

Why?

Why?

Why?

My spirit wants to know

Could I have prevented this?

Where is he?

Is she okay?

Who's next?

Could it be worse?

I wasn't strong enough.

What's happened to me?

I've turned into _____

A PRAYER FOR PEACE OF MIND

PLEASE HELP ME!

I CAN'T STOP REMEMBERING...I LIVE THROUGH IT ALL OVER AGAIN.

DID I DO THE RIGHT THING?

WHAT IF _____

_____

_____

I CAN'T BELIEVE THE DOCTORS DID ENOUGH _____

_____

_____

I WAKE UP IN THE MIDDLE OF THE NIGHT WITH MY BRAIN RACING, GOING OVER IT AGAIN _____

_____

_____

PLEASE. I NEED SLEEP. I NEED PEACE.

From your inner child: Write a letter to God
or the universe from you as a 5-year-old.

GUILTS & REGRETS

GUILT…the "if only" of grief.

"If I had not asked him to go to the store…
the accident would not have happened."…

"I asked her to go to the doctor to have it checked
and the next thing I know she is in the hospital
and dying…."

"It's my fault, I should have known better…"

We believe that we are the cause of the
death. We could have or should have
been able to change the circumstances….if only…

Guilt is not always rational. But it is real.
We often feel guilt in grief. It is our way to try to

manage the loss of control that we feel. If we can blame ourselves then there is a reason… a why… to something that often has no reason.

Guilt is difficult to predict or to control. Even if you know intellectually that you are not guilty,,, you still feel it emotionally.

Sometimes it simmers silently in your heart and mind and eats at you constantly. Sometimes you let it out and are reminded by others that you could not change things.

Don't let others place guilt on you…. you can do a good enough job of this on your own!

REGRETS…the softer side of guilt

"I wish I had told her more that I loved her"…

"I never remembered her birthday with a card
or flowers"…

"He said he loved every one of the ties we bought
him….I wish I had taken him to a ballgame
instead"…

"I would hug him, and hug him, and hug him….
even if he said he didn't like it"…

We look back and realize that there are many
times we missed an opportunity to tell someone
how much we cared for them….and it saddens us
to know that we wasted precious time that we will
never have again.

The pangs of regret are lessened when we say....

"I WILL NEVER LET THOSE MOMENTS, THOSE OPPORTUNITIES TO SHOW HOW MUCH I CARE, SLIP BY ME AGAIN. I WILL FIND THE WORDS AND THE WAYS TO SAY "I LOVE YOU" SO THAT THEY CAN HEAR IT AND KNOW."

Do you have any regrets that need to be acknowledged? Do you need to change how you let time slip away without saying what is in your heart?

GUILTS AND REGRETS
Fill in your shoulds, gottas, maybes and oughts.

I USED TO LIKE THE QUIET... NEVER SEEMED TO HAVE ENOUGH

Quiet time.

Now, it hangs so heavy

on my hands.

I need some noise.

I need some conversation.

I need some people to be with..

But I also need to be careful and make
sure the doors and windows
are locked.

Put the alarm system on.

Lock the car doors.

Have flashlights and batteries
within reach.

And always have my cell phone
battery charged.

I need to talk with someone but I need to
be careful who I talk to.

Strangers sometimes seem
to listen better than my own family.

I must be careful that I do not
say something to a stranger
that will lead to danger.

But, I also need to think about
making some new friends.

From different places....

Support groups, church, classes,
new volunteer activities.

You are not here...and you are

supposed to be...you should be.

Home is/was my sanctuary but

I don't like coming home to

an empty house.

Thank God for the dog...I can talk to her

And she is glad to see me...I must

remember to give her food and water.

Your pictures mock me.
Why are they here and you are not?

TRICKED BY TIME

How time changes after a death.
The ticking of the clock
– it's slower today than normal.
Why do you suppose that is?
Time hoodwinks us.
The hours are creeping by.

But when I look over my shoulder
to yesterday and before,
the days, the years seem to have flown by.
Where did the minutes go.
It always seemed to take so long to get there
– to get to those special days
– to reach the age of being admitted
to more privileges, grown-up expectations.
But that time really just whooshed by.

We filled those moments, you and I.
We crammed so much living into those days.

But empty hours march so slowly
– and the clock is ticking, oh . . . so . . slowly.
Or so it seems.

People write books about time management.
They think time can be made to flow evenly
– properly used, with life balance and goal setting.

Grief teaches another lesson.
Sorrow has its own clock.

TIME
TOO MUCH
NOT ENOUGH
There's room for your notes

	IS MY FRIEND	CAN BE MY FRIEND	IS NOT MY FRIEND
SLEEP			
DRINKING			
EATING			
TV			
MOVIES			
GAMBLING			
RETAIL THERAPY			
EXERCISE			
COMPUTER GAMES			
INTERNET			
iPHONE			
OTHER			

HOW DARE YOU!!

How DARE you leave me!

You left me alone here.

You left me to handle a lot of things
I don't want to handle.

You left me to cope with a lot
of things I don't want to cope with.

Now I have to deal with all this stuff
and, worst of all, you're not here.

That's the worst. You're not here.

The "mad at you" and "missing you" are all
jumbled up inside me and I can't even think straight.

I want you here. I need you here.

What am I going to do?

The Ambush

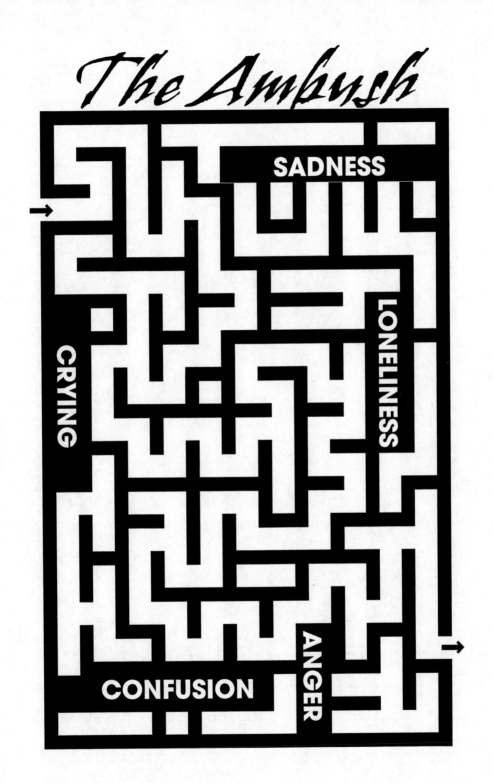

SADNESS

LONELINESS

CRYING

CONFUSION

ANGER

I'M SO ANGRY AND I DON'T KNOW WHY...

I'm angry at _____

because_____

_____

_____

_____

_____

when _____

_____

_____

Prayer for Breath

Some moments I can't breathe.

I feel like someone has stolen the very air around me and that I am suffocating in my grief.

Help me feel the air and take a breath.

The thought of you not being here with me takes my breath away and I feel like I am drowning.

Give me air to breathe and light to see that I will get through this dark and fearful place.

I want to feel you next to me and know that we are together. Life without you is taking my breath away.

Let me learn how to breathe without you.

Deep Secrets!

[unmentionable grief feelings]

Admit it. You have thoughts and feelings that you wouldn't for the world share with anybody. We all do. That is especially true when you are grieving for someone. In death, that person wears a halo. BUT maybe you know otherwise. You may have some unmentionable feelings, especially now.

In this book, at least, you get to acknowledge the whole truth. In these pages you have permission to see, to explore and to feel the reality of your world.

If you find yourself anywhere on these pages, you are SO normal. We'll never tell.

MORE DEEP SECRETS!

We stopped being in love a long time ago.

That doctor could have saved him/her.

I wish I could have been the one to die.

Watch out for the mailman.

I have a broken heart and you're complaining to me about your broken dishwasher.

Those EMT's didn't try hard enough to save him/her

I have some family members I can't stand right now.

I walked into the room and smelled her perfume.

He came to me in my dreams last night and told me he's okay.

MORE DEEP SECRETS!

MORE DEEP SECRETS!

I reach for him in the bed at night.

I keep her unlaundered nightgown in a plastic bag. I bury my face in it just to smell her again.

I hear him calling to me.

She came to me in my dreams last night and we made love.

Take your @#%&@ talk about angels and go . . .

My arms feel so-o-o-o-o empty.

I saw him coming toward me out of the corner of my eye.

My life is so much better without you.

I can't tell anybody this.

They wouldn't understand and
I would be too embarrassed.

My deepest secret _____

_____

_____

_____

My darkest regret _____

_____

_____

_____

My sense of anguish because_____

_____

_____

_____

**REMEMBER: This is your book. You can keep or rip
out any page you want.**

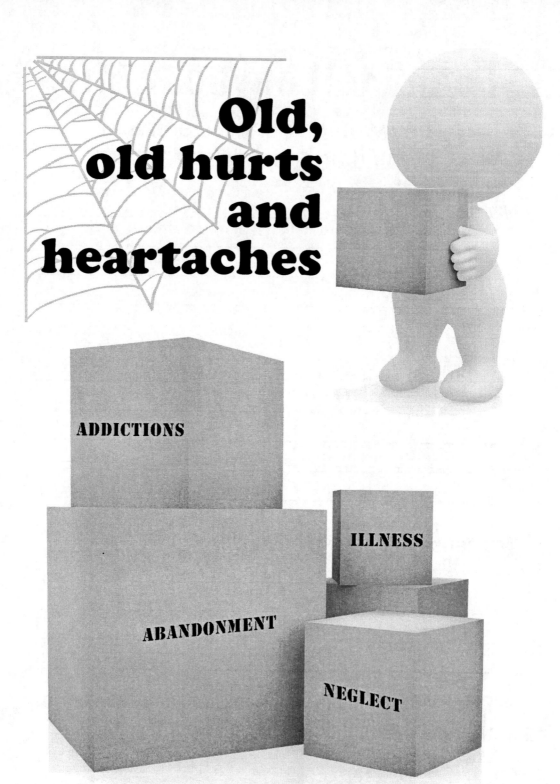

Old, old hurts and heartaches

ADDICTIONS

ILLNESS

ABANDONMENT

NEGLECT

I don't even want to think about what's in that box. It still hurts too much. Your death makes it hard to forget right now.

I could never make you understand what you did to me, and now it's too late.

How can I ever forgive you?

WHIRLPOOL OF LOSS

LOSS

LOSS

BUILDS CHARACTER

FEELS LONELY

ADDS UP

IS HARD WORK

CREATES FEAR

CHANGES HOPES AND DREAMS

CAN NOT BE COMPARED

HAPPENS TO EVERYONE

TAKES TIME TO HEAL

CHANGES EVERYTHING

CAN BE CREATIVE

HAS LONG LASTING EFFECTS

SOME RIPPLES IN THE POOL

CANNOT BE COMPARED

"Who hurts the most?" Is your pain worse than hers? Does her loss trump yours?

It doesn't work to try to compare your loss with others. Each loss is its own loss. Only some circumstances change. And pain cannot be measured or compared.

CREATES FEAR AND ERODES TRUST

The big question is always "Can it happen again? Will it happen to someone I love? Could it happen to me?" We want the assurance that the people left in our lives are safe. We no longer trust that nothing bad will happen. It can be a frightening and helpless feeling .

IS CUMULATIVE (ADDS UP)

If you've been through a loss before, you should get through this one easier. Right? WRONG!! It doesn't get easier. In fact, with each loss, you will re-live and re-grieve all former losses.

CAN BE CREATIVE

What will I have to learn to do that I don't already know how to do? What adjustments do I have to make to my world? How different will things become? How will I make it work? Will I choose to become bitter, or will I become better? Will I stagnate, or be creative?

CHANGES HOPES AND DREAMS

Now I need a new vision of the future. So much has changed. What am I going to do now?

? YOUR WORLD WAS OUR WORLD

The world turned upside down after your death. I'm not sure now where I belong in it, what part of it is still mine, what part is gone with you, where, when or how the rest will hold together without you.

Some days when I look around I realize that I'm stuck here with things I hate. I've hated them forever, but because you liked them they stayed. Now they are here but you are not.

I don't know if it is morning or night. The days are dark and the nights are endless. Time has a different definition: Before your death and After your death... **BD and AD.**

There are moments that seem endless and yet the days are just flowing by...even though I want time to stop, to go back, to be when we were together. Just the thought of being together makes me happy ... then sad. I feel angry. I feel confused. I feel like crying at every little thing. If I laugh I feel guilty. How can I possibly laugh with you gone?

Is this you today? ☐ **Yes or** ☐ **No**

This morning your dog made a mess. I hate the dog right now, but he was your best friend. He made a mess because I don't remember the  last time I took him for a walk. Feed him, feed me, feed the birds….

FEED ME!

WALK ME!

PLAY WITH ME!

I don't want anything or anybody relying on me right now. I can't even remember to comb my hair and brush my teeth. Now I have to feed the dog… and he wants to play!!! I just want to go to bed and pull the covers over me and wake up with you.

How do I do the things you used to do around here….I wish I would have paid more attention when you were here. Did I ever tell you thank you for all that you did do?

You were never supposed to die first. GOD, how

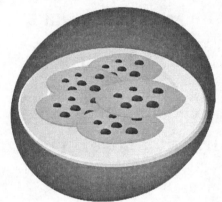 could you let this happen to me…to us. My world… I don't want it to be my world…I want it to be our world again.

People come with casseroles…with cookies…with fruit baskets…I can't eat them…I wish they would come with a dinner invitation or an offer to stay for dinner…help me eat some of this food.

_____

Is this you today? ☐ Yes or ☐ No

And yet, today I ran out of cereal, coffee and milk. I hate going to the supermarket now. The cereal aisle is the worst. I look at your favorite and I start to cry. How do I start to live this different life. I don't want to....

I think about you all the time. Sometimes more in death than in life. Why? So many why, why, whys that never seem to get or give an answer. God and I are not on speaking terms right now. Yet, I want to talk to him and tell him he let me down. I wanted a miracle.

I'm angry at everyone and everything. And I think I'm jealous when I see people who are together….in their world, and families that are complete.
That used to be me.
That used to be us.
I don't want to be just me…
I want to be us again.

Is this you today? ☐ **Yes or** ☐ **No**

OUR WORLD IS NOW...

I make lists and lose the lists.

> Where did I put the car keys?

I found them last night in the refrigerator.

> Am I going crazy?

You would have said…"you didn't have far to go!"

I can hear you say it. I look around but you are

not here.

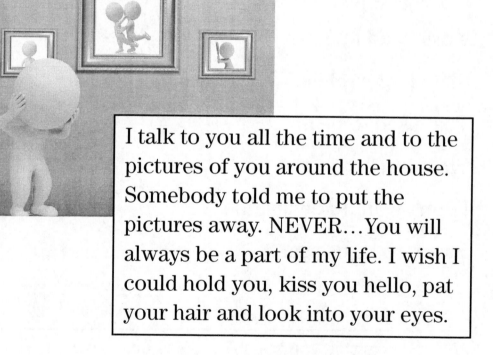

I talk to you all the time and to the pictures of you around the house. Somebody told me to put the pictures away. NEVER…You will always be a part of my life. I wish I could hold you, kiss you hello, pat your hair and look into your eyes.

I have to pay the bills, write checks and make telephone calls about your insurance. I looked at the signature on the check...I can't even recognize my name... is this really me without you....????

The last call I made, they were curt and rude. How dare they. Don't they know that I 'm grieving?

No, I guess they don't know. But I want them to know and I want them to make my world right. How dare they refuse...

Some children came to see me today. They brought me some flowers and giggled as they played with the dog.

What do children know about the sadness of death?

What do children know about death?

Is this you today? ☐ **Yes or** ☐ **No**

Then one little boy said, "My Grandpop died a year ago. We used to go fishing a lot. I haven't been fishing since he died. I really miss him." I guess children know more about death and sadness than I thought. I'm learning more about my world every day. I miss you, too, and I always will.

MY WORLD

I have to go to the bank. Every time I'm in the car a song comes on and I start to cry. Memories are bittersweet. Driving and crying, living and dying. My world is so different now. Things I never thought about are at the top of the list.

I see and hear and live differently now.

Someone complained about the rain. I thought of you and how you liked rainy nights. If I could just listen to the rain with you I would never complain again.

A friend said the good news and the bad news is that I will survive. Sometimes I want to...most times I don't. I think nasty thoughts. I say nasty things...mostly in the mirror but sometimes they slip out to people....and the dog.

Someone visited me today and I was so busy telling them about my sadness that I didn't even offer them something to eat or drink...all those cookies sitting on the table and I didn't.

Is this you today? ☐ **Yes or** ☐ **No**

What has happened to my social niceties…what has happened to my niceties….any niceties in my world.

My world……. Not your world….or our world, is calling. I have to attend a wedding…and another funeral…

I have thank you notes to write and some telephone calls to make.

Oh yes, I also have to feed and walk the dog.

Is this you today? ☐ **Yes or** ☐ **No**

Prayer for Inner Peace

I have never felt so uneasy with myself. So confused. So unaware of others. Only my grief is important to me. Who have I become?

Give me the peace to understand that I am in turmoil and that I can weather the storm.

My world is upside down and so am I. I don't care about any of the things that once were so important to me.

Help me learn to adjust to this new me who is emerging from the grief.

MY WORLD
before loss

What memories do you cherish?

Write a memory for each space.

My Social World

The World We Shared

My Inner World

and after loss

What is changed?

What is left?

What is yet to be?

EVERYTHING CHANGES
"THAT OLD GANG OF MINE"

I wonder if they'll invite me to his family reunion?

Do I still have a place at the Thanksgiving table?

Will I still see the stepchildren?

I mean to keep in touch with the cousins, but,

honestly, I probably won't.

The neighbors talk to me differently now.

I don't have anyone to go to the movies with.

My friends seem distant.

SOME THINGS
NEVER CHANGE
"GETTING TO KNOW YOU"

The kids have been so supportive.

Who knew how kind my neighbors would be?

I heard about this support group.

I know I'm not ready to emerge yet, but someday
I will be.

The cards keep coming –
friends old and new.

GRIEF & YOUR SPIRIT

It has been said that "all loss is loss of self."
Here's how that works and why it hurts:

You are a complex being with
many facets (faces) and each
relationship with people, pets,
possessions or places evokes a
new and unique *facet* in you.

You already knew that when
you were very young. You were

different with
grandparents than with parents;
and you had other *faces* for
teachers and for playmates.
That's just the way we are.

So when someone or something is lost to you, so is that part of you – your special face for them.

The connection which has roots in your spirit is ripped from you and, if the roots go deep, the pain can be enormous. We call those roots "attachment."

Attachment is a powerful force that binds us to each other. Love grows out of attachment. Courtesy, compassion, a sense of belonging, spirituality, religion, patriotism, sexual passion and the desire to have children – all of these and more spring from

attachment – "the ties that bind" and the faces that we show to each other.

So when an attachment is broken, a face is lost. Eventually a new facet of you will develop for that relationship – one based on memory and longing and a keen awareness of how much you have lost.

…and the loss can touch surprising parts of you. Such as some of these:

(There's room for you to write about it if you care to.)

body_____

mind _____

spirit _____

competence _____

health_____

- energy _____

- mood _____

- soul _____

- finances _____

- social nicieties _____

- sexuality _____

- relationships_____

- faith _____

- organization _____

- hopes and dreams _____

- hygiene _____

- appetite _____

- connections _____

- rationality _____

cleanliness _____

joy _____

affection _____

empathy _____

tolerance _____

Can you add to this list?

_____

_____

_____

Prayer for Hope

I am unsure of tomorrow because
you are not here to show me
the way and come along with me.
All I see ahead is darkness.

**Help me believe that tomorrow
will be better than today.**

There are so many things I need
to do to just keep even in my
everyday world and I know keeping even is only the beginning.

**Let me be happy keeping even and
not worry about getting ahead.**

I want to stay put...no...I want
to go away...I want to talk...no...
be silent...I want to hide and not
come out until I know who I am
and where I am going.

**Help me find the way without
you.**

TUG OF WAR

MOURN THE OLD

I DESPERATELY MISS YOU TODAY.

I'M REMEMBERING OUR LAST SHOPPING TRIP. YOU FELL IN LOVE WITH SOMETHING. I SAID WE COULDN'T AFFORD IT.

YOU ALWAYS LIKED GOING TO CHURCH/TEMPLE.

BUILD THE NEW

I NEED TO GO
GROCERY SHOPPING.

I HAVE TO WRITE A CHECK
FOR THE ELECTRIC BILL...
I WISH WE HAD BOUGHT
WHAT YOU WANTED.

THEY WERE LAUGHING AT
SOMETHING IN THE SERMON
TODAY BUT I COULDN'T LAUGH.

TUG OF WAR

MOURN THE OLD

I CAN'T THINK STRAIGHT.

I CAN'T GET
INTERESTED IN
READING ANYTHING.

HOW YOU LOVED THE YARD.

I DON'T WANT TO GET UP.
I WANT TO HIDE HERE
IN THE DARKNESS

BUILD THE NEW

I HAVE TO GET READY FOR WORK.

I HAVE TO DECIDE WHAT TO DO ABOUT THOSE INSURANCE PAPERS.

NOW I HAVE TO MOW THE GRASS.

I NEED TO TAKE A WALK OUTSIDE AND GET SOME FRESH AIR.

LET IT OUT!

PEOPLE SAY "You have to let it out" and you don't know what that means: Well, give it a try. There's a lot of pain in you.

Here are some things people do:

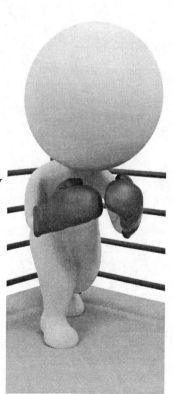

- saw wood

- hammer nails

- knead bread – or clay – or play dough – or your pillow

- punch a punching bag

- shovel dirt

- run

- do push-ups

- scream – deep down

- talk and talk and talk and talk
- clean things like closets, ovens, floors
- throw things – listen for the shattering sounds
- walk the dog
- scream again
- write about it
- draw pictures

Don't do these things:

- drive too fast

- punch holes in the wall

- overeat or starve yourself

- shop – shop – shop

- take your anger out on others

- hook up with strangers

Don't hurt yourself. At a time of excessive stress, it's not unusual to become accident prone. Be careful not to fall, not to cut or burn yourself, not to run into things. Take your time.

Don't use drugs or alcohol to avoid the pain. It won't work and grief cannot be safely avoided if we expect to recover.

Don't use prescription drugs for the same reason. They just mask and delay the pain. Headaches can be cured. Grief cannot.

Have you heard of the primal scream? It's a scream that comes out of deep anguish. Has your crying ever ended up in screaming?

Don't be afraid to scream – a scream that comes from down deep inside you – as deep down as your pain.

Sometimes there's a harmony between your spirit and something else – the car motor, the vacuum cleaner, the lawnmower, the radio – and you can use that harmony to let a deep scream well up and find its way out.

Imagine you're a lion letting out a deep roar that just naturally arises from the fierceness of your life right now.

My lion needs to roar today because

_____

_____

_____

_____

_____

_____

_____

_____

_____

_____

_____

TAKING CARE OF ME
SO THAT I LOOK GOOD.

I don't feel like messing with
me right now
I just want to be left alone
I just want to go out for lunch
or dinner
I want company
I want to be alone

I need to clean out the closets....

not just yours, but mine as well....

I will never be the same person

that I was before

That's scary....

Who am I now?

Who am I going to be?

I don't know what I want...
I want you here with me.

Thank God for the cat....

I can talk to her

And she is glad to see me....

I must remember to give

her food and water.

HIS

I should get a haircut.
I need a shave.

Must remember…deodorant, comb hair,
try to look and smell good –
such an effort right now.

I was noticing, some of my ties
are out of date, and nobody wears
that kind of suit anymore.

I should throw away those
old polyester suits, and the
tee shirts and underwear
with the holes…

Maybe I
should grow
a beard.

Hers

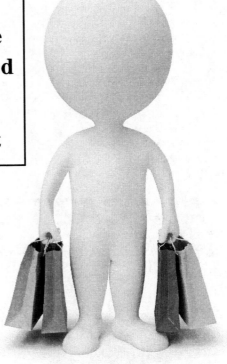

Do I need a new do? Hair color? Perm?

My wardrobe, my hair style, my scent – All the things I thought mattered now seem different…

…because I'm different

I'm not sure how to put myself together anymore – such an effort right now.

My hands look awful. I need a manicure.

AS I GAZE IN THIS MIRROR,

Who do I see?

How am I being changed?

Do I look as fragmented as I feel?

The Ambush

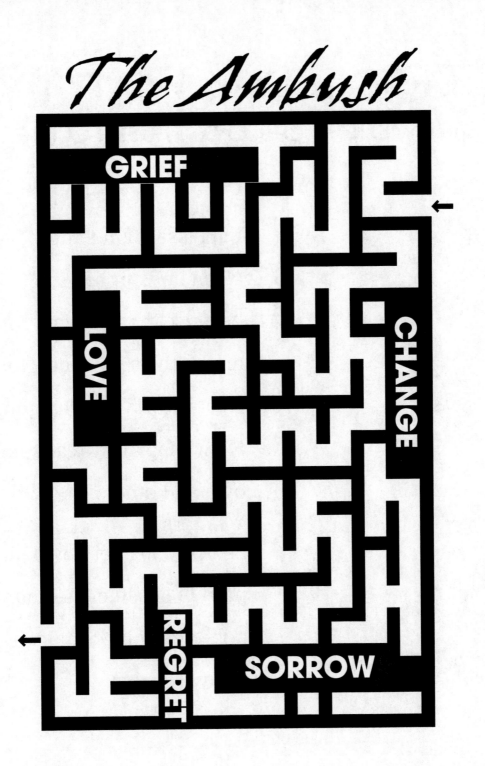

GRIEF

LOVE

CHANGE

REGRET

SORROW

The Pity Party
Why did you do this to me?

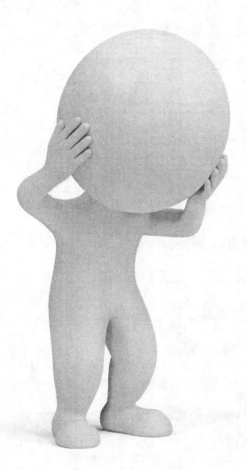

I'm pissed. I'm left to clean up your mess, because the one who dies is the lucky one. No estate work. No clean-up. No wiping away tears, my own and others.

Self-pity. My very own pity party! I deserve one and nobody's going to take it away from me!

I've been robbed and it turned my whole life upside down (He used to do all this. Now I have to) or (She knew how to run all this stuff. I don't).

So who comes to a pity party? You can't come. You aren't here.

Do I invite fear, anger and guilt to the party? If I don't invite them, will they gate-crash and come anyway?

What am I afraid of? I don't even want to think about what it's like to die and be dead. Just living is trouble enough.

Nobody understands.

WHERE DID THE YEARS GO?

HIS PARTY PREP

(Fill in what you need for your party)

_____

_____

_____

_____

_____

_____

_____

_____

_____

_____

_____

_____

_____

_____

Her Party Prep

(Fll in what you need for your party)

_____
_____
_____
_____
_____
_____
_____

_____
_____
_____
_____
_____
_____

Your Ambushed Spirit

Who was this JOB guy?

Talk about ambushed! Have you heard about Job?
His name comes up every time the question of
suffering comes up:

Why do good people suffer?

Why do bad things happen?

JOB is the story in the Bible of a righteous man
who was tested to the limit.

He lost his children, lands, buildings, crops . . .

Naturally enough, he had a few questions:

"What did I do to deserve this?"

"Why me?"

His 'friends' said, "You must have done SOME-THING wrong."

His wife said, "Curse God and die."

Job said, "Shall we receive the good at the hand of God, and not receive the bad?"

Then 35 chapters of questions and laments and human reasoning . . . .

. . . followed by 4 chapters of God grilling Job:

"Where were you when I laid the
foundations of the earth?"

    "Have you given the horse its strength?"

    "Can you unbuckle Orion's belt?"

-- challenging questions like that.

Finally, Job, awestruck, humbly worshipping
and wiser, with his fortunes restored, still has
no answers, but he has gotten the point.

What points can we get? Here's a start:

• God, or the universe or life doesn't owe us any
  answers and doesn't owe us protection either.

- If you weren't there at the beginning, can't give the wild things their strength, and can't reach up and rearrange the stars, then you probably wouldn't understand any of the answers anyway.

- Why do you think you deserve miracles? Be honest.

- There's a lot to be said for "walking humbly with your God."   Be at peace.

What are your unanswered questions?

IT'S DARK AHEAD . . .

"What am I going to do now?"

"How can we get through this?"

When you experience a shattering loss, it's normal to have a total sense of unreality. The future is dark and you can't see the road ahead.

And in this gloomy environment you have things you have to do: contact people, make plans, make decisions, accept the reality of what has happened, find ways to go on.

Grief is hard work. Some have said it is the hardest work of our lives. You have to let yourself believe what you don't want to believe – to acknowledge

that it really happened. And you have to let yourself feel the pain of your loss.

There is no road map for this dark road –
except the love of family and friends and keeping
on keeping on – one step at a time, one day,
one minute at a time.

In the process, you may discover that the
darkness that seems so threatening, can also be
a kind of gift – a place to wait. A "time-out" place
where you can be exempt from many other
demands and expectations. A place to begin the
heavy work of grieving.

Don't be afraid of the dark.

"Light cannot

see inside things.

That is what the dark is for:

Minding the interior,

Nurturing the draw of growth,

Through places where death

In its own way turns into life."

from *"For Light,"* (first verse) in *The Book of Blessings,*
To Bless the Space Between Us, by the Irish poet,
John O'Donohue Doubleday, New York, 2008.

The Ambush

RESENTMENT

IF ONLY

DENIAL

GUILT

SHOCK

Grief through the ages
FIND THE AUTHORS OF THESE WORDS ABOUT GRIEF

1. The dew of compassion is a tear

2. Tomorrow will be a new day…when God sends the dawn…he sends it for all.

3. The soul would have no rainbow, had the eyes no tears.

4. While I thought I was learning how to live – I have been learning how to die.

5. The last day does not bring extinction but a change of place.

6. Yes, he thought, between grief and nothing, I will take grief.

7. Death is an eternal sleep

8. The saddest moment in a person's life comes only once.

9. I don't think of all the misery, but of the beauty that remains.

10. The bitterest thing in our today's sorrow is the memory of yesterday's joy.

11. From happiness to suffering is a step; from suffering to happiness is an eternity

(If you get them all, you read too much!)

Grief through the ages

____ a. A Jewish proverb

____ b. Kahlil Gibran 1883-1931

____ c. Brendan Francis

____ d. William Faulkner 1897-1962

____ e. Cicero 106-43

____ f. Lord Byron 1788-1824

____ g. John Vance Cheney 1848-1922

____ h. Leonardo da Vinci 1452-1519

____ i. Joseph Fouche 1763-1820

____ j. Anne Frank 1929-1945

____ k. Miguel de Cervantes 1547-1616

Answers:
a=11, b=10, c=8, d=6, e=5, f=1, g=1, h=3, i=4, j=9, k=2

129

"A CONVERSATION
with the UNIVERSE"

We start very young making sense of life. We

absorb and learn from our world as we decide:

What kind of a place is this?

Am I safe? Can I trust people?

Am I okay? If not, how do I get okay?

Can I make my own choices?

What is good and what is bad?

Can I learn and grow?

All our life we are answering more questions

and making sense of life. We decide

Who's in charge here?

Who am I?

Why am I here?

What do I value? What matters?

What is expected of me?

Can I risk loving and being loved?

Can I share myself with future generations?

Am I doing the best I can with my life?

What do I believe in?

Who or what has a claim on my life?

Human beings, like you and me and everyone else, can be described as these three things:

- meaning-makers
- control seekers
- pain avoiders

So that means

- we want our world to make sense and give us significance;

- we want to control our world, and

- we want to be happy and pain-free.

Sounds good, doesn't it?

But what happens when grief enters your life?

- Suddenly things don't make sense;

- you feel helpless and

- it hurts like crazy.

No wonder there are more questions!

We are searching for meaning and order and peace. Check out the questions on the next page.

"An **ARGUMENT** with the **UNIVERSE**"

When we are ambushed by loss and pain, we have more questions to ponder:

• Why do bad things happen?

• Why to me?

• Where is she now?

• Is he okay now?

• What happens to us next?

• Who is in charge here? Do I believe in God?

• Do I believe in a God who cares about us?

• Do I believe God took him/her from me?

• How much control do I have over my life?

• Can I survive? Can I thrive?

Can I let myself feel the pain of loss?

Who am I going to be now?

What's my fault?

What's my responsibility?

What can I be sure of?

What do I do with this pain?

Why pain? Why death?

Where do I direct my gratitude?

Do I have any gratitude? Should I?

Where do I direct my anger?

Do you wrestle with the questions on these pages?

Which questions don't trouble you at all?

Which questions are gnawing at you today?

What other questions are on your list?

What would you like to say

back to the universe right now?

YOU ARE A CHILD
OF THE UNIVERSE,
NO LESS THAN THE TREES
AND THE STARS;
YOU HAVE A RIGHT
TO BE HERE.
AND WHETHER OR NOT
IT IS CLEAR TO YOU,
NO DOUBT THE
UNIVERSE IS UNFOLDING
AS IT SHOULD.

FROM THE DESIDERATA
BY MAX EHRMANN

PRAYER FOR PATIENCE

Lord, I need a truckload of patience, please.

They're telling me things I don't believe.

"She's in a better place."

"God needed another angel in heaven."

"She had a good life."
(Like she's had her share)

"You'll get over this in no time."

What better place than here with me, and besides, you have enough angels. I can't believe you would steal mine. Why couldn't she keep on having a good life here? And I don't believe I ever will get over this.

I know they mean well, but I just want to deck 'em when they say things like that.

Lord, I need a truckload of patience, please.

All this and GRIEF TOO

There may be factors in your life or your world
that are keeping you from dealing with your loss
and your grief.

Here are some examples;

- If you lost someone by

    suicide

    homicide

    accident

    disaster

    random freakish event

    warfare or terrorism

These factors can block grief or make it complex
or complicated.

- If you are a bereaved parent
- If you or someone you care about caused the loss
- If you are a secret griever
- If you yourself are seriously ill
- If you suffer from depression or mental illness
- Other overwhelming issues

Grief can make dealing with these additional issues even more difficult.

We strongly urge you to get to a support group or a professional counselor. Don't put it off.

Prayer for Perspective

I try to remember that there are other people hurting worse than I hurt.

I try to remember there are tragedies and catastrophes and atrocities all over the world and not just here in my little corner of it.

There are millions of people grieving millions of losses.

But I don't care about any of them today.

I just hurt so much right now, that's all that seems real.

Forgive me, World. Maybe I do care. I can't ache for you today. Maybe tomorrow.

If Your Sexual Partner Died, this Page Is for You...

Because Your Sexual Being Did Not Die.

MEN	WOMEN
I'm so horny, I could...	Why do I have to look for anyone else?
Does it still work?	Will anyone ever love me like that again?
I miss just holding you	

The emptiness of grief is compounded by the loss of familiar, comfortable sex. You need to grieve a whole relationship and all of its parts.

Because the loneliness really hurts, you must be very careful. Watch out for the predatory lovers, the lounge lizards, the wolves in sheep's clothing, the red hot mamas, and sometimes even the casserole ladies. Because of your loss and your need, your emotional judgment may be impaired. Your "I know better" is broken.

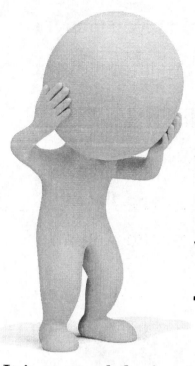

If Your Loss Was Not Your Partner, But Loss Has Disrupted Your Sex Life,

This Page Is for You.

It is normal during grief for sexual drives to diminish. It may also feel like a betrayal to enjoy anything, especially sex, at this time.

It is very normal for partners to differ on this.

- Men are likely to use sex to feel okay.

- Women are likely to need to feel okay before they can enjoy sex.

This difference can create tension at any time, but when you are in grief, all tensions are magnified. Other angers may ambush you as well because anger is bound up with grief.

Therefore it is easy for a wall to come between you. On the other hand, there is no time when you have a greater need for physical closeness and intimacy.

The courage and determination to keep your communication open is the key to making it through together.

MONEY FOCUS

Finances: what to pay, what not to pay, who to trust, who can help …

If you are in charge of the finances, it's important that you keep solvent at a time when you might be least able to focus or make good decisions.

Ordinarily you don't need any advice. But right now is different – you're not quite yourself. So we offer some tips and suggestions in case you need them – and don't assume you won't. There will be days . . .

• Beware of untrustworthy people who can enter your life at this time. Many predators, who sound so good, do not have your best interests at heart.

> *"Exercise caution in your business affairs; for the world is full of trickery."*
> *(from the Desiderata, by Max Ehrmann)*

- Beware of anyone pushing you to make a quick decision about a purchase.

- Do seek professional help from trusted and reputable financial institutions and advisors if you need it.

- Do not surrender <u>complete</u> control of your financial environment to anyone.

- If possible, do not make major expenditures or financial commitments for at least a year.

- Do not move your residence unless you must for at least a year (two years is even better).

- If you want to express gratitude for services or kindnesses received at this time, we suggest you delay any large financial gifts or commitments for at least a year. Your heart wants to say 'thank you' but your head needs to think it over. Take time to reflect. Impulse giving can be unwise.

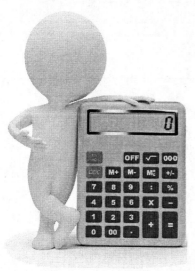

- Maintain your customary level of charitable giving if you can.

- Be sure to pay your taxes, monthly bills, utilities, insurance, credit cards, car payment, rent or mortgage. Make a list and check it weekly. Or use the checklist on the next page.

Enlist a trusted family member or friend to remind you and perhaps assist you.

- Don't postpone that trip you really want to take, or that new car you badly need, but, beware of "retail therapy" – trying to ease the pain by buying something, getting something new or going somewhere interesting.

- Beware of the internet and bar scene – there are serious emotional and financial dangers out there.

- Get more involved in your financial health and well-being.

Bills, Bills, Bills – a Checklist

Here's a three-month table to track payments

Bills, payments due	Usual Due Date	1st Month	2nd Month	3rd Month
Mortgage or rent				
Condo/Assoc. dues				
Car payment -1				
Car payment -2				
Utility – gas/elec.				
Utility – water svcs				
Phone – 1				
Phone – 2				
TV				
Internet				
Cleaning Service				
Lawn Care				
Pool Service				
Credit Card – 1				
Credit Card – 2				
Credit Card – 3				
Donation/pledge				
Medical bills				
Other – taxes, insurance, loans . . .				

Help with Money Woes

HAVE YOU THOUGHT:

I don't know what to do.

I don't know where to begin.

I just want to walk away from all this.

I need help.

TAKE A DEEP BREATH.

You may not feel able to take charge of your affairs right now. BUT don't wait to be rescued.

TAKE IT ONE STEP AT A TIME.

Get the best advice available.

Consider asking a trusted friend or relative for assistance.

Whatever you do, make sure it's legal.

Don't be afraid to ask for help.

- If you do not have income now, or you can't access your money, get help as soon as possible from assistance agencies in your area. Look for them in the blue government pages of your phone book or on line.

If in doubt, in the U.S., start with the Ombudsman. This is a state office that can respond to just about any question you have.

In addition, churches/temples, funeral directors, banks, credit unions, Veterans' Affairs, Consumer Credit Counseling Services, local social services are possible places where you may get advice and resources for your financial needs.

- Beware of agencies and businesses that want to sell you financial products or services. They can be costly and may not have your best interest at heart.

"Let me know if I can do <u>anything</u> for you."

You will hear that many times. They mean it – sort of. Some don't really expect you will ask for something specific. Others would be delighted to be able to help if they only knew what to do. Let them help. Grief is hard enough without trying to go it alone.

If you are the kind of person who enjoys giving help but is reluctant to ask for help, now is the time to let yourself be on the receiving end. Make a list – or use the one on the next page – to let people know some of the things they can do that would really be appreciated.

If you are the kind of person who is able to receive as well as you give, a list can zero in on the things that you need and might forget to ask for in the moment.

Of course, there are things you should not delegate. For example, in your need for help, don't compromise your privacy – especially financial and medical information.

On the next page is a list – complete it, copy it, and hand it out to those kind souls who offer to help and really mean it.

HELP! HELP! HELP!

Thank you for offering to help. I've checked some items on this list and I would be glad for your help if you see something there you would like to do for me.

____ Go to lunch or dinner with me

____ Come visit – spend some time

____ Exercise or walk together

____ Go to church or temple with me

____ Help me write the thank you notes

____ Help me take the car in for maintenance

____ Help me with some light cleaning

____ Grocery shopping (list and cash provided)

____ Rides to appointments

____ Laundry

____ Mowing, weeding, trimming, watering

____ House sitting or pet sitting

____ Sorting mail

____ Other _____

____ Other _____

____ Other _____

Only you can find the light at the end of your tunnel...

There are days that you don't see the tunnel, let
alone a light at the end of it.

There are mornings that hearing the birds
sing sounds like an insult. And rainy days are becoming
welcomed friends.

Gloomy is a description you like. Sunny and bright don't
have much of a place on your calendar.

24/7 for you pertains to how you feel all the time...SAD
AND LONELY.

**But even grief has to take a break. One morning
you wake up and the sun is shining into the room
with such force that you want to shut it out....but it
won't go!**

You become aware the month has marched on
and you couldn't stop it...the pages of the calendar
just kept turning.

LIFE continues to flow on...even if you want
time to stand still, it can't and it won't.

And you realize that you are caught in the tunnel and part
of your grief journey is to work your way through it and
eventually out into the light and the land of the living.

But you don't want to go......

Not yet...

Help me find the light at the end of my tunnel...

Help me to do the hard work of grief

and to allow the sadness and the hurt

to show me that love lives on

and walks with me

in this dark place.

I don't know what is up ahead,

or just around the corner

and that's why I can't think about going there just yet.

The future seems so bleak.

Help me to believe that it will get better

and that I will see the light at the end of the tunnel.

THE 7 A's OF GRIEF WORK ©

ACKNOWLEDGE

Admit the reality that the loss has happened.

ARGUE

Struggle with the emotional reactions
caused by the loss.

ADJUST

Recognize that you are changed and
circumstances around you are also changed.

ATONE

Resolve the regrets and guilts that accompany loss by being able to say "I'm sorry," I have learned from this situation.

ACCEPT

Understand the unfairness of loss and realize that forgiveness is an important part of the process.

ASSIST

Use your resiliency to support others as they go through the grieving process for their losses.

ACCOMPLISH

Recognize that you have the ability to go from victim to survivor and from survivor to striver and from striver to thriver. To be, to do and to make a difference.

Grief through the ages
FIND THE AUTHORS OF THESE WORDS ABOUT GRIEF

1. It matters not how a man dies, but how he lives.

2. Those who living fill the smallest space, in death have often left the greatest void.

3. The first requisite for immortality is death.

4. Yesterday I loved, today I suffer, tomorrow I die; but still I think fondly, today and tomorrow, of yesterday.

5. One must lose one's life, in order to find it.

6. Of the many evils common to men, the greatest of all is grief.

7. The mind is its own place, and in itself can make a heaven of hell, a hell of heaven.

8. What does not destroy me, makes me strong.

9. Suppressed grief suffocates.

10. There is a remedy for everything, it is called death.

11. When God shuts a door, he opens a window.

12. Everyone can master a grief, but he that has it.

13. Grief teaches the steadiest minds to waver.

Grief through the ages

___ a. William Shakespeare 1564-1616

___ b. Sophocles 495-406

___ c. John Ruskin 1819-1900

___ d. A Portuguese proverb

___ e. Ovid 43-18

___ f. Friedrich Nietzsche 1844-1900

___ g. John Milton   1608-1674

___ h. Menander 342-292

___ i. Anne Lindbergh 1906

___ j. Stanislaw Lec 1909-1966

___ k. G. E. Lessing 1729-1781

___ l. W. S. Landor 1775-1864

___ m. Samuel Johnson 1709-1784

Who are these guys anyway?

Answers: a=12, b=13, c=11, d=10, e=9, f=8, g=7, h=6, i=5, j=3, k=4, l=2, m=1

FAMILY

First of all, no two people in the family grieve alike.
For example, you might notice the following:

– Men grieve more with their muscles than women do.

– Women talk about feelings more than most men.

– Younger children grieve and play, grieve and
  play, question and play, cry and play.

– Older children may share feelings with
  peers rather than adults.

– College students are at the greatest risk for delayed grief
  and risky behaviors.

– Siblings and Grandparents are often the forgotten grievers.

– Pets grieve too.

Second, the pain of grieving is complicated by the frustrations and responsibilities of life that continue to place demands upon all of us. We may end up angry, irritated, hurt, self-focused, withdrawn and/or overly anxious. A household filled with these emotions can be difficult to live in, to say the least.

If this sounds challenging, you're right. Loving and open communication are essential for your family at this time.

PRAYER FOR A DIFFERENT KIND OF STRENGTH

Isn't it true that "the family that weeps together, keeps together?"

Someone told me I need to be strong for the family. What they meant was I shouldn't cry, or show my feelings. I should hold it in. Let them think I'm a solid rock so they can think their world is safe. The trouble is I'm not a rock and they would know that's phony. And I don't think it would make them feel safe. I think it would make them feel alone.

I'm not sure that keeping a stiff upper lip is the best kind of strong. Or at least it's not the kind of strong I want my family to learn. Please give me a different strength. Let me open my heart to the people I love. Help me to let them see and feel my pain so they can feel safe to let me see and feel theirs. Give us each the strength to sorrow together and support each other, especially now.

I know we won't all grieve the same way, and some days we might not like each other very much, but we are each missing someone like crazy. Give us the kind of strength to do the missing and the grieving and the weeping together.

CHILDREN GRIEVE

Children grieve. Children miss the people and things in their life that disappear. They seldom understand WHY. It is usually mysterious and scary. (Sounds a lot like how we sometimes feel in our grief.)

We are often asked to explain to them what we ourselves are seeking to understand...at a time when we have the fewest words and perhaps no explanations.

Children ask three questions…not always in order and not always with words.

They ask:

WHO WILL TAKE CARE OF ME NOW?

Because they are egocentric in their thinking this is often the first thought that comes to them.   Can be asked in ways that we may not recognize…such as….Who is going to take me to the ball game now that grandpa is not here?

DID I DO ANYTHING TO CAUSE IT?

Guilt is a strong reaction to grief. It has to do with feeling totally out of control and if I had a part in causing it…then I have some control in the situation and maybe I can do something else to change what has happened.

Regrets are things we wish we had done differently and we can learn from them and do things more positively the next time…and honor the person who is no longer here.

Regrets are a learning tool in grief for children and for us.

CAN IT HAPPEN AGAIN...
CAN IT HAPPEN TO ME?

One of the most important parts of this question is...can it happen to me? It is the child's first look at mortality and it can be very frightening. It is a time to assist children with the idea that everything eventually dies and that how we live is truly important. Also, children need to know that they will have someone to care for them if someone close to them does die.

DO THESE QUESTIONS SOUND SIMILAR TO THE ONES WE ASK...ONLY NOT SO BOLDLY AND NOT OFTEN ALOUD...

Other questions that will come out...

WHERE DID THEY GO?
CAN I GO TOO?
WHEN WILL THEY COME BACK?
WILL I EVER SEE THEM AGAIN?
WILL THEY GET HUNGRY OR THRISTY?

For very young children a short explanation of death that is helpful...

Death is when the body stops working.

SOME SUGGESTIONS FOR CHILDREN WHO ARE MISSING THEIR FRIENDS, FAMILY OR ANIMALS

Write a note to the someone you miss.

Draw or Color a picture.

What do you remember about them? Tell or write a story .

Its OK to be SAD   MAD   UNHAPPY but it is not OK to hurt someone or to hurt yourself

It's Ok to eat yummy stuff that makes you feel better, but healthy food is better for you

It's OK to be afraid...

It's not OK to hurt yourself

Try to remember....(yeah I knew that)

Don't drink and drive...drugs don't help

Take care of your own grief before trying to help others (like putting on your oxygen mask first....)

School is still very important

Yes, you do have to take that math quiz....

Write the lyrics to a song about the death or write a poem to the person who died

What music groups speak to you?...think of friends who can understand and listen

Think about friends you can trust

Who can't deal with it? Who needs to see you happy?

Who can you talk to who will let you cry or get angry?

Remember to love and take care of your animals

MATCH UP THE FACES
AND THE SENTENCES

playing a game together

feeling like I don't have
your love anymore

something we
laughed about

feeling sad because
everyone is so sad

you remembered
my birthday

holiday dinners

the sound of your voice

wondering if I made
you go away

having someone
to love me

MATCH UP THE FACES AND THE SENTENCES

a time I was mad
at you

going to the movies
together

a time you were
mad at me

getting hugged

a bad feeling I can't
talk about

just having you around

missing you so much

coming home and
you are not here

being scared about
people dying

CHILDREN'S PRAYER
GETTING THROUGH THE CHANGES THAT HAPPEN IN GRIEF

Why do I feel so different than I did before they died?

Is it OK to feel different because I am going through something called grief?

Help me with these new feelings

But I don't like these new feelings…they make me sad, and mad and sometimes scared. I want to make the feelings go away. I want my life to be the way it was before.

Help me learn to feel more comforable with these feelings and the way things are now.

I don't know if I will be able to remember all the things we did and all the fun we had…I can't remember the sound of your voice. Memories matter to me.

Help me never to forget you.

I am afraid that things will get worse and that I will not be OK. Change is scary.

Help me have hope for a brighter future.

I ask why this has happened but no one gives me a good reason. I guess that sometimes there is not a good answer.

Help me to understand that sometimes "why" does not have an answer.

Sometimes I'm not sure who I am and where I'm going or who I am going to be, because the person I love is not here to help me. Is it OK to feel lonely and wonder about who you will be?

Help me to know that there are wonderful parts of my mind and body that will grow as I grow.

MEANING-MAKING IN THE MIDST OF BROKENNESS

Grief hits you in your mind and your soul.

Your mind on grief has hard work to do.

It's hard work letting in the truth that this

is really happening.

It's hard work letting yourself feel the pain – hurt.

It's hard work adjusting to the changes that are being forced on you or that you have to choose.

It's hard work finding out how to go on and how to create your new world.

Your soul on grief has hard work to do.

It's hard work trying to make some meaning out of what has happened.

You have to wrestle with the questions:

Why did this happen to me, now?

What can I do about it?

It's hard work recognizing that my identity had changed.

Who am I without you?

Who am I going to be?

It's hard work trying to find some benefit in what has happened.

I'm hoping I can adapt and grow.

Mind and soul have been battered.

The physical bond is broken; touching is gone.

The way you always thought it was and the way you hoped it would be is gone.

What is expected of you is changed; roles are shifting and uncertain.

But some of what we think is broken may still be intact, even if changed, even if the pain is great. But the bond, the love, the presence, the spiritual connection, the history, are still intact.

Yes, grief is very hard work. The good news (and maybe the bad news) is that you can survive.

CONTINUING BONDS:
A NEW UNDERSTANDING IN GRIEF

When there is a death, the relationship changes but it does not die.

We still have conversation with those who have died. We talk to their pictures, we sit with them at the cemeteries, we wear their jewelry and their clothes, We see their mannerisms and personality in their heirs.

We reach out to initiate a connection to them by visiting and remembering their favorite places, and we are supported by the knowledge that they are always with us in spirit and at the heart of all we do.

The bond that we shared in life still continues after death because love never really dies. It is held together in spite of grief by the love and life we shared.

...THE LOVE GOES ON...

There are those who assume that with a death, you must start over without that relationship. But experience and evidence suggest otherwise.

We do grieve for what once was and is now gone, changed and different.

But there are some signs of continuing bonds that are evident as we sit down with family and someone says something in an old familiar way and someone else says...."you said that just like he/she always said that." That's a sign that the person who has died has become a part of you.

Has this ever happened in your family?

_____

_____

When you wear their favorite piece of jewelry you feel an identification with them. You take on some of their traits and sometimes even feel differently about some issues then you did before they died.

Do you have jewelry, china, furniture, clothing that connect you to someone who has died?

_____

_____

They become a role model as you do some things you have never tried before. You see their face in your mind's eye and know that they are with you especially in a time of crisis.

Have you ever asked them for help?

_____

_____

Continuing bonds provide comfort and support. They allow a continuity between the past and the present which helps the future look a bit brighter.

We grieve, we remember, we connect again in a deeper spiritual way that allows them to remain always in our hearts.....CONTINUING BONDS.

*Gradually, you will
learn acquaintance
With the invisible form
of your departed;*

. . . .

*And be able to enter the hearth
In your soul where your loved one
Has awaited your return*

All the time.

from "*For Grief,*" in *The Book of Blessings,*
To Bless the Space Between Us, by the Irish poet, John O'Donohue
Doubleday, New York, 2008.

A SALUTE TO VALIANT MOURNERS

SURVIVORS OF THE UNBEARABLE

THERE ARE THOSE WHO

CARRY SCARS SO DEEP,

WOUNDS SO TENDER,

MEMORIES SO HORRIFIC,

AND LIVES SO SHATTERED

THAT WE WONDER HOW THEY GO ON.

BUT MANY DO,

CHOOSING LIFE,

EVEN FINDING LOVE,

STILL WILLING TO MOURN AND REMEMBER.

WE HONOR YOU.

Loss, Grief and Renewal
by Toni Griffith, LCSW

Loss

YESTERDAY, TODAY and TOMORROW
It hurts in the place where my YESTERDAY used to be.
And now my TODAY is empty and forever changed.
And the TOMORROW I want will never happen.

Grief

PAST, PRESENT and FUTURE
The PAST resurfaces and says, "I wish I would have…"
The PRESENT calls back, "If only I could…"
While the FUTURE sits silently,
refusing to be seen or heard.
But with hope, with resilience, and with all the long
steps on the pathway, we reach the place of

Renewal

THEN, NOW, YET TO BE
I look at THEN and choose to remember the best.
And NOW I let the smiles carry me through.
So that I can look forward to what is YET TO BE.

The Road Ahead

The road of grief is often long and painful and it seems that everyone wants to give you a map and a promise for your journey based on what they have experienced.

However, you are the traveler. You are the map-maker for your own journey.

Thank you for allowing us to travel part of the road with you.

As you continue,

  may peace surprise you

   on your way.

Our hearts go with you.

Toni and Ellie

Grateful Recognitions

We want to express our gratitude to all the forerunners in grief theory for their insights into the human experience of loss, grieving and life transitions. Your ground-breaking work has given us a body of knowledge that has opened up worlds of awareness and understanding and focused our compassion. It is in part due to your work that this book has emerged.

Early influences for us were two writers in particular. Edgar N. Jackson, D.D.: his pioneering work, Understanding Grief, published in 1957 and considered a classic in its field, laid the groundwork for the current approaches to grief and grief management. Orville E. Kelly wrote Make Today Count, published in 1975. Written in response to his terminal illness, it is a moving salute to living as well as a tender farewell.

We want to make special note of the following theorists and the concepts they have contributed to our thinking: J. William Worden, Ph.D. and Therese A. Rando, Ph.D. for the tasks of grief; Kenneth J. Doka, Ph.D., for disenfranchised and gender issues in grief; Alan D. Woolfelt, Ph.D., Charles A. Corr Ph.D. and Donna M. Corr, R.N, M.S, for children's concepts in grief; Phyllis R. Silverman, Ph.D., Dennis Klass, Ph.D., and Steven L. Nickman, M.D., for continuing bonds; Robert A. Neimeyer, Ph.D., for meaning-making; Thomas Attig, Ph.D., for the concept of brokenness; and the author Mitch Albom for the concept of continuing relationships.

The Book of Blessings, To Bless the Space Between Us, by the Irish poet, John O'Donohue (1956-2008) is published by Doubleday, New York, 2008.

John Greenleaf Whittier, the American Quaker poet who wrote *Maud Muller* quoted on our *If Only* page, lived from 1807 to 1892.

American poet, Max Ehrmann, author of *Desiderata*, written in 1927, lived from 1872 to 1945.

Quotes from the Biblical book of Job are from the *New Revised Standard Version*, published by World Publishing, Grand Rapids, Michigan, 1989.

An enormous vote of thanks goes to our graphic designer, Michelle Helfrich of MH Design Company, LLC whose designs not only captured and interpreted our meanderings, but also inspired continuing creative ventures.

Thanks to Karen Hodges Miller of Open Door Publications, LLC who found us wandering in search of a publisher and set our feet on a clearer path.

And thanks to our many loved ones who have endured our struggles to take a great body of theoretical knowledge and put it into a manageable guide for those who have been *ambushed by grief*.

Toni and Ellie

TONI GRIFFITH, LCSW

Is a practicing grief therapist from Medford, NJ. She spent many years in hospice as a bereavement counselor as well as working with over 10,000 school children with grief issues. Toni has a puppet show on grief and transition and has also written a book on grief for children, "Good Grief, It's Sky Blue Pink," and has written several articles on grief and loss and also on pet loss.

She has received the national The Heart of Hospice award, along with her son, Devin Griffith. She has also been named Woman of the Year in Burlington County, New Jersey. She assisted with emotional support at Liberty State Park following 9-11 and has also assisted at the AIDS quilt showing in Washington, DC.

She works with special populations of grievers: very young children, children of incarcerated parents, victims of domestic violence, developmentally disabled adults, traumatized grievers, disenfranchised grievers and those whose grieving is complicated or stalled.

Toni came into her own world of grief by becoming an adult orphan, a grieving widow, a bereaved parent, a grieving friend and a hospice companion. Toni believes that every death teaches its own lesson about life.

REV. ELOISE A. COWHERD, M. DIV.

Ellie Cowherd played in a lot of cemeteries as a kid (a preacher's kid, that is) and learned that loss and grief are a normal part of life. A pioneering book, *Understanding Grief*, by Edgar N. Jackson, D.D., sparked an interest in the processes and challenges of grieving, gave rise to a term paper in Seminary, and launched an informal specialty within her ministry calling. Her congregational and hospital years have sharpened this focus and brought her into contact with bereavement specialists in religious, health and hospice programs. But it has been the day to day realities of loss – all kinds of loss – experienced by congregants and hospital patients, as well as her own losses, that have taught the understanding beyond words. Their pain, taken too lightly by a frenzied world, asks to be taken seriously and to be cared for. This book is a part of her answer.

She is a graduate of Princeton Theological Seminary in Princeton, New Jersey, and is an ordained minister with The Presbyterian Church, USA. She currently is Consultant for Congregational Life with the Presbytery of West Jersey and has also worked in several pastoral positions in churches in the South Jersey area.

She has been the Manager of Pastoral Care at Virtua Memorial Hospital, Mount Holly, New Jersey, and was a founder and on-going leader of Basic Grief, a support and professional growth group for bereavement specialists. She was a recipient of the Woman of the Year Award in Burlington County, New Jersey.